TO MY SONS

TO MY SONS
LESSONS FOR THE WILD ADVENTURE CALLED LIFE

BEAR GRYLLS

LION

Published by arrangement with Alpha International.
First US edition published by David C Cook
ISBN ISBN 978-1-4347-0358-3

This edition published by Lion Books
an imprint of
Lion Hudson plc
Wilkinson House, Jordan Hill Road,
Oxford OX2 8DR, England
www.lionhudson.com/lion

ISBN 978 0 7459 5601 5

First edition 2009

Acknowledgments

Unless otherwise noted, all Scripture quotations are taken from the Holy
Bible, New International Version®, NIV®. Copyright © 1973, 1978, 1984
by Biblica, Inc.™ Used by permission of Zondervan. All rights reserved
worldwide. www.zondervan.com. Scripture quotations marked NCV
are taken from the New Century Version. Copyright © 1987, 1988,
1991 by Word Publishing, a division of Thomas Nelson, Inc. Used by
permission. All rights reserved. Scripture quotations marked NKJV are
taken from the New King James Version. Copyright © 1982 by Thomas
Nelson, Inc. Used by permission. All rights reserved. Scripture quotations
marked NLT are taken from the New Living Translation of the Holy
Bible. New Living Translation copyright © 1996, 2004 by Tyndale
Charitable Trust. Used by permission of Tyndale House Publishers.

Cover design: Amy Konyndyk
Front cover photo © Bear Grylls Ventures, edited by Jonathan Roberts
Back cover photo © Bear Grylls Ventures
Illustrations: Charlie Mackesy

A catalogue record for this book is available from the British Library

Printed and bound in Great Britain, September 2012, LH26

PREFACE

To my sons, the great joy in my life.

This little book is a culmination of all that I have learned about the game of life. I have learned these simple truths through many mistakes and many falls. I have learned them from watching and being around those I love and admire, and I have learned them through the hard times that life sometimes throws at us.

I have also learned that what I value most is found close at home: just being with you three boys and your mama.

I hope these simple truths help you blossom in the game of life, and I hope they help you follow your hearts and many dreams. I hope they remind you to cherish those close to you and to live boldly and with a smile.

You are the most wonderful joy in both our lives, and I could never have imagined such good fortune to be able to hold you close to me so often (although it never seems enough!).

I adore you and am oh, so proud of you. You are the best.

With love,
Papa

Aim to live a wild, generous,
full, exciting life – blessing
those around you and
seeing the good in all.

———

Follow your dreams –
they are God given.

Have a few close friends who
you see often – their friendship
matters more than having
many shallow acquaintances.

———

Be honest and vulnerable with
those close to you.
It creates strong bonds.

Don't be held back, either by fear or by lack of confidence. Go for it, despite these very normal emotions that we all feel occasionally.

Build people up.

Be faithful – any old
slime can cheat!

Smile and laugh
more than is
considered normal!

Be loyal – it is the
mark of a man.

Remember the verse, "We are the sweet smell of Christ among those who are being saved and among those who are being lost."

(2 Corinthians 2:15 NCV)

Exercise at least every other day – make it a habit. Then you will shine even brighter.

Choose your job
carefully – do work
that excites you. It is
where you will spend
so much of your time.

"Another dull day at the office"

Don't be afraid to be weak occasionally.

Choose a job that
betters people's lives.

Snack on nuts and fruit
– they suppress appetite
and make you strong!

———

Remember the verse, "I
can do all things through
Christ who strengthens me"
(Philippians 4:13 NKJV).

Cheerfulness in adversity
is a key character trait
in the game of life.

Moments of doubt
are part of life. Accept
them and remember
that Jesus Himself said,
"My power is made
perfect in weakness"
(2 Corinthians 12:9).

Nobility is not a birthright – how we act in the big moments defines who we are.

"Thank you, your majesty"

Encourage, encourage;
help, help.

Remember this verse by heart:
"Even there your hand will
guide me, your right hand will
hold me fast" (Psalm 139:10).

———

Understand that failure is
an essential stepping-stone
on the road to success.

"Ok, so this puddle
is to be avoided next time"

Always keep the big picture in mind – you are greatly loved by Jesus and your job is to love Him and others in return. The rest is detail.

"That's a big picture"

Give more than you take,
especially with friends and
family. See the best in people –
as Christ does with you.

———

Compliment people – kind
words can change lives,
and people rarely forget.

Manners really matter;
in fact, they make
the man.

Remember that how you speak about others speaks loudest about yourself.

———

If you want to see the real man, give him power over people and see what he does. Remember this in how you treat people.

Be the most enthusiastic
person you know!

————

Love Jesus.

————

Find a fun, honest, down-to-earth
local church and support it.

Be gentle.

———

Consider others better
than yourself.

———

Be especially kind, thoughtful,
and generous to those who
are overlooked in life – this is
the measure of a real man.

Pray daily – what a person the Lord is to have helping you!

———

Be courageous in key moments.

Eat lots of fruit and vegetables. They fight all the free radicals that try to slow you down.

Be kind to those whom
others neglect.

———

If supply is short, then look
for something to give away. It
is a law of the universe – to
receive you must first give.

Put 10 per cent of your income aside and give that money to those in need – whether friends or charities. You have the power to save lives.

"Merry Christmas...
Ten chocolates, so you
have to give me
one"

Speak generously
about people.

Sometimes it is
worth losing a battle
to win the war.

Jesus came to seek
and to save us – let
Him do His job!

Help friends in need.

———

Don't lend money; rather, give it.

Say "why not?"
rather than "why?"

Generally in life, try to leave five minutes too early rather than five minutes too late.

The people to be nicest
to in life are your wife
and your children — give
them the most time,
energy, and love, and
you will be happy.

Spend more time with your family and less at work – no one on their deathbed says they wish they had spent more time in the office!

Marry only for love.

This is a great one to remember: "And be sure of this: I am with you always, even to the end of the age" (Matthew 28:20 NLT). I had this engraved on Mama's wedding ring when we married!

———

Lead by example.

"walk this way, please"

Preach Jesus every day – when necessary, use words! That is, love and listen to people.

No one cares how much
you know until they know
how much you care.

———

Don't lie.

You have two ears and one mouth – use them in proportion: Listen twice as much as you speak!

Don't one-up
people's stories.

"But remember the Lord your God, for it is he who gives you the ability to produce wealth" (Deuteronomy 8:18).

Thank God for your many blessings; then go out there and blossom. It is okay to succeed!

Always look people
in the eye.

Have a firm handshake.

When you call someone, first ask if it is a good time to talk.

Don't be afraid to be quiet
and let others shine.

————

Treat others as you would
like to be treated.

"Here's a Cake...
Now where is mine?"

Be extra cautious
if mixing business
with friendship.

Pride comes before a fall – so don't be too proud to let others win. There is room for everyone to do well!

Be ambitious – think big and take calculated risks.

" we'd like a large loan...

for a chocolate factory "

Be open, honest, and
fair in all your dealings.

It is okay to be weak —
with less of you there is
more room for God.

———

When you're right, shut up, and
when you're wrong, admit it.

Many great people
over the centuries have
depended on their
faith – it is a sign of
great strength to need
Jesus in your life.

Be the first to apologize.

Enjoy the silence.

Make a little time to
be quiet by yourself
every day and just be.

Don't go to battle
unless it is absolutely
necessary – to turn the
other cheek takes great
strength and courage.

"Here's my other cheek."

Crying is healthy!

———

Always hold hands with
those you love whenever
you have the chance.

———

Gratitude, gratitude, gratitude.

Relax. You have no need for the common concerns of life. Remember Isaiah: "The LORD will guide you always" (58:11).

———

Don't worry about anything that is outside your sphere of influence – if you can't change it, don't waste time worrying about it!

Learn a few clean jokes
and a good card trick.

Laugh at yourself.

Learn to play an
instrument.

Swim in streams.
Be spontaneous – it's fun!

——

Watch a sunrise occasionally.

Bet your life on Jesus.
Ultimately that's the big one!

———

Make people smile every day.

Know that I love you
and am always with you
and am oh, so proud.
— Your Papa

———

"The LORD himself
watches over you!"
(Psalm 121:5 NLT)